Jesus for today

ok is ... re ... before
las ...

Chris Wright

OXFORD UNIVERSITY PRESS 1996

D1439397

About the series

We live in a world where there are people of many different religions. In many of our towns and cities Buddhists, Christians and Jews live alongside Muslims, Hindus and Sikhs. If you travel abroad, you will soon experience whole countries that have been shaped by religion.

We all have different ways of looking at things. It could be said that we all see the world through our own "spectacles". These spectacles are made up of our beliefs, opinions, attitudes and values. What is important to you might not be important to me.

Religious people see the world through their spectacles, which affects the way they see and live in the world. We can't understand someone else's worldview unless we look through their spectacles. The *Religion For Today* series helps you to do this by giving you the skills and knowledge to understand people with beliefs different from your own.

In learning about another religion you will also be given the chance to think about your own life. So you will not only learn about the religions you study; you will also learn from the religions.

Chris Wright, Series Editor

About this book

Many people believe that Jesus is one of the most remarkable people who ever lived. He was a Jew who lived 2000 years ago. He was born in a small town in what is today called Israel. He was not really famous in his own day, but his influence has spread down the centuries and throughout the world. His followers, called Christians, can be found all over the globe. Many non-Christians admire his teaching and the way he lived. In this book you will learn about his life, his teaching and the world he lived in.

There are a number of paintings in this book from all over the world. You will be asked to look at the paintings and try to get behind them to what the artist is trying to say. You will notice that some artists have painted Jesus as a black man, others as an Asian, others as a white European man. This also says something about beliefs in Jesus. Artists throughout the world have tried to explain how they believe Jesus speaks to the different situations in which people find themselves.

Practical hints

- Words you may not be familiar with are explained in the text. You can also check their meaning in the Glossary at the back of this book (page 62).
- We learn about Jesus from the Bible. The first part of the Christian Bible is called the Old Testament; the second part is called the New Testament. There are a number of references in this book to the Bible. A reference will look like this:

Matthew 5:17.

In this reference:

Matthew is the name of the book. You will find a list of the books of the Bible at the beginning of the Bible.

5 is the number of the chapter. In the Bible the chapter numbers are printed large.

17 is the number of the verse. The verse numbers are printed much smaller.

- Dates are given as CE (in the Common Era) or BCE (Before the Common Era). Jesus was born in about 6 BCE.

CONTENTS

ONE

HO IS JESUS?

Is there anyone or anything you would be willing to dedicate your life to, even to the point of death? In this unit you will be examining what some people have said about Jesus and why they consider him important. Many have been willing even to die for him.

1 *Before you start studying about Jesus, collect what you know about him on the blackboard.*

"No one single person has influenced the world as much as Jesus of Nazareth." This is a claim believed by millions of Christians down the ages who are followers of Jesus Christ. His influence can be seen today. A third of the world's population is Christian. For example, a hundred years ago there were no churches at all in Korea. Now that country has the largest church in the world with a congregation of 410,000. Sunday services run one after the other throughout the day to fit everyone in.

But why is Jesus so important? Who do people believe he is? One writer described Jesus in the following way:

2 *(a) Find five positive claims which this statement makes for Jesus.*
(b) Name three things Jesus did not have. Why do you think the writer mentions these things?

> 66 Jesus Christ was born in Bethlehem almost 2000 years ago. During his first thirty years he shared the daily life and work of an ordinary home. For the next three years he went about healing sick and troubled people and teaching small groups in villages, in the fields and by the lakeside. He called twelve ordinary men to be his helpers. He had no money. He wrote no books. He commanded no army. He wielded no political power. During his ministry he never travelled more than 200 miles in any direction. He was executed by crucifixion at the age of thirty-three. Yet over 900 million people throughout the world now worship him as God. 99

People who met Jesus held a number of different opinions about him.

"Unless this man came from God, he would not be able to do a thing."
(John 9:33 – a blind man healed by Jesus)

"The man who did this cannot be from God, for he does not obey the Sabbath law."
(John 9:16 – some Pharisees)

When a group of teenagers were asked what they thought about Jesus they gave the following answers:

"He never existed."
   (Robert)

"Jesus was a remarkable man but was not God."
   (Matthias)

"Who cares who he is anyway?"
   (Kai)

"A good man."
   (Lydia)

"A wise teacher."
   (Samantha)

"He was the Son of God."
   (Jessica)

3 Which of these statements about Jesus do you
(a) most agree with, and
(b) least agree with?
Explain why.

4 Carry out your own research into what people today think about Jesus. Interview five people on their views about Jesus. Encourage them to explain their views.

5 A twelve-year-old pupil asks, "Why do we have to learn about Jesus?" Use this unit to provide this pupil with at least two reasons for finding out about Jesus.

"This is Jesus, the King of the Jews."
(Matthew 27:37 – written on the cross)

"We know that he really is the Saviour of the world."
(John 4:42 – some Samaritans)

"This man was really the Son of God!"
(Mark 15:39 – a Roman army officer at Jesus' crucifixion)

"You are the Messiah, the Son of the living God."
(Matthew 16:16 – Jesus' disciple Peter)

TWO

PICTURING JESUS

Cameras didn't exist at the time of Jesus. No one knows what he looked like. His earliest followers do not seem to have been interested in his appearance. They were much more concerned with who he was and what he had come to do. Artists have painted Jesus in ways which make sense to them. In China Jesus is shown as Chinese, in Africa he is an African, and so on.

The picture on the left is The Light of the World *by an English artist, William Holman Hunt painted in 1853. It illustrates a passage from the Bible. See if you can find it in the last book of the New Testament – Revelation 3:20. What do you think this verse means?*

Eastern Orthodox Christians use pictures like the one above to help them during worship. Such pictures are called "icons". In what ways do you think pictures might help during worship?

Part of a twentieth-century painting of Jesus from Cameroon, West Africa.

A Chinese painting on silk of Jesus and Mary Magdalene. This may illustrate a story from Matthew 26:6 – 12 – see if you can find it.

1 If you were to draw a picture of Jesus what would he look like? What would he be doing? Would there be any objects in the picture? If so, what? What background would you choose? Explain why.

2 Imagine that you saw one of these pictures in an art gallery on holiday. Write a postcard home about it. How would you describe it? What feelings come to mind when you look at it? What is the artist trying to say about Jesus in the picture?

3 Christians believe that Jesus was both a human being and the Son of God.
(a) Choose a picture which shows that Jesus was human. Explain how the artist shows this.
(b) Choose a picture which shows Jesus as the Son of God. Explain why you chose the picture and how the artist shows this.

4 Imagine a younger pupil says she doesn't believe the four pictures are all of the same man. How would you explain to her that they were all pictures of Jesus? Write a short paragraph.

THREE

WHAT DO NON-CHRISTIANS THINK OF JESUS?

In this unit you will be discovering some of the views of people from other religions about Jesus.

Although only Christians believe that Jesus was the Son of God, many people from other religions have strong opinions about him.

> ❝ Jesus was an unorthodox rabbi [teacher] of his time. Jews do not believe that he was the Messiah. They do not believe that he overcame sin and death. ❞ *(Yehazkel Landau)*

> ❝ Hindus fully accept, with Christians, that Jesus is God Incarnate [in the flesh]. Hindu religious tradition speaks of many incarnations. Christ is the power of God expressed on earth in human form. ❞ *(Swami Bhavyananda)*

> ❝ Sikhs have come to acquire the greatest respect for the teachings of Jesus Christ, especially the Sermon on the Mount. ❞ *(Indarjit Singh)*

Mahatma Gandhi (1869-1948) was a devout Hindu and is regarded by many as the father of his country, India. He led the Nationalist movement against British rule and was well known for his doctrine of non-violent protest. He wrote:

Mahatma Gandhi leaving India to visit England

> 66 What, then, does Jesus mean to me? To me, he was one of the greatest teachers humanity has ever had . . . in Jesus' own life is the key to his nearness to God; that he expressed, as no other could, the spirit and the will of God. It is in this sense that I see him and recognise him as the Son of God. 99

> 66 All Muslims acknowledge that Isa (Jesus) was a prophet and a messenger of God. His virgin birth, his miracles, especially his power to raise the dead, and his purity are also generally accepted. 99 *(Michael Nazir-Ali)*

1 When Christians talk about the Incarnation they mean the Son of God took on human flesh and became part of our history. Look at the quotations. Which other religion also believes that God can take on a physical body and visit the earth?

2 (a) Muslims believe Jesus was one of the prophets sent by God. What do they not believe about him that Christians do?
(b) Look at the Jewish view about Jesus. Does it agree with the Muslim view?

3 Gandhi was not a Christian, yet he thought Jesus was one of the world's greatest teachers. One of the main principles of Gandhi's life was non-violent resistance to bad governments. He said non-violence was "good-will towards all life. It is pure Love." What might he have learned from Jesus about this? Look up Matthew 5:38 – 48. Explain in your own words what Jesus was teaching. Do you think Jesus' teaching is realistic?

FOUR

THE MESSIAH

1 *Imagine what life would be like if this country were ruled by a foreign power. Perhaps we had lost a war and the invading forces took over everything. How would it make us feel about our country? In groups decide what you would do (e.g. would you just accept the situation or would you plan to fight against it? how?).*

Do you know?

The word "Messiah" comes from a Hebrew word. It means "anointed"– that is, a person chosen by God for a special task. The Greek word for "Messiah" is "Christ".

Dreaming of the Messiah

Palestine had been ruled by foreign powers for over 300 years by the time Jesus was born: firstly by the Greeks and then by the Romans. A number of Jews looked forward to a time when God would send his Messiah to free them. Some thought he would be a descendant of David, who had been King over them in the tenth century BCE. He would lead the Jews in the battle against the Romans. Some thought that the Messiah would have special powers from God. There would be one final last battle at the end of the world. God would then re-create everything. There would be a reign of peace (Isaiah 11:6).

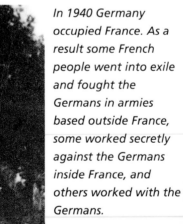

In 1940 Germany occupied France. As a result some French people went into exile and fought the Germans in armies based outside France, some worked secretly against the Germans inside France, and others worked with the Germans.

A group of Essenes lived in the caves at Qumran near the Dead Sea. This is one of the caves in which scrolls written by the Essenes were discovered in the 1940s and 1950s. The monks lived a simple life under strict rules and had frequent ritual baths to purify themselves.

The Essenes

These were Jews who lived apart from others and prepared themselves for the coming of two Messiahs: a priestly one and a political one. It is thought there were about 4000 of them. They are not mentioned by name in the New Testament, but we know about them from other writers and from the discoveries at Qumran (look at the photograph). Those who lived in the desert were obeying the words of the prophet Isaiah: "Prepare in the wilderness a road for the Lord!"

The Zealots

The beginnings of the group can perhaps be traced to a Jewish patriot, Judas of Galilee, who in 6 CE led a revolt against the Romans. They hated being ruled by a foreign power and refused to pay taxes to them. The Romans thought of them as terrorists. They saw themselves as freedom fighters. They were an underground movement who wanted a Messiah to lead them in battle.

> **2** Many Jews were looking forward to a Messiah who would re-create a better world. In your opinion what three improvements to the world would make it a better place?

> **3** How do the following verses in the Old Testament (the Jewish Scriptures) describe the Messiah: Isaiah 9:2–7, Ezekiel 37:24–5 and Isaiah 11:1–9? Design a WANTED MESSIAH poster using these texts to find out the credentials which the Messiah should have.

The Pharisees

These Jews followed God's law, found in the Scriptures or handed down by word of mouth, very closely. Most of the teachers of the Law were Pharisees. They disliked Roman rule but didn't believe in violence to overthrow it. They hoped for a Messiah who would be a descendant of King David, who would come and rule them when the people had been taught to live better lives. Change would be brought about by God.

Was Jesus the Messiah?

Jesus' closest disciples came to believe that he was the Messiah. When Jesus asked Peter who he thought he was, Peter answered: "You are God's Messiah." (Luke 9:20). Jesus then taught them that he was not the sort of Messiah whom the Jews were looking for. Instead of overthrowing the Romans with physical power, he was to be rejected and "put to death, but three days later he will be raised to life" (Luke 9:22).

FIVE

THE WORLD OF JESUS

In this unit you will be thinking about the different groups of people in society and then consider the different groups at the time of Jesus.

> **1** Sometimes there is conflict between different groups of people when they disagree.
> (a) Which people in the picture are shown clashing? What do you think they are disagreeing about?
> (b) Which other group might clash? How? Why?

Name the different groups of people in this picture.

At the time of Jesus the society in which he lived was made up of a number of important groups as well as ordinary people – both Jews and non-Jews. Sometimes these groups disagreed and clashed. In the last unit you read about the Essenes, Zealots and Pharisees. In this unit you will find out about the Romans and those who supported them.

The Romans

The Romans ruled the country, although they allowed local princes to run everyday affairs in some areas. They allowed the Jews a little power through a religious council, the Sanhedrin. This council controlled religious matters and had some power over criminals.

Herod's family

King Herod the Great was allowed by the Romans to rule the Jews for almost forty years, until his death in 4 BCE, a short time after Jesus' birth. His kingdom was divided among his sons, with Roman approval, but some of their lands came to be directly ruled by the Romans.

The Sadducees

This was a small but very powerful and wealthy Jewish group. Many of them were priests who worked in the Temple in Jerusalem and they dominated the Sanhedrin. The high priest was chosen from their families. The Sadducees compromised by working with the Romans. They were anxious not to upset them since it was the Romans who allowed them to hold such power.

3 *Using this unit and the previous one, write a newspaper headline for each of the following groups of Jews which captures how they responded to the Romans: Sadducees, Pharisees, Zealots, Essenes, supporters or members of Herod's family.*

This is a map of Palestine at the time of Jesus. Find Jerusalem, Nazareth, Capernaum and Bethlehem. Copy the outline of this map on a large sheet of paper and these four places. Then find out which of these places was the following:

▶ *the place of Jesus' birth*
▶ *the place where Jesus grew up*
▶ *Jesus' base when he was teaching in Galilee*
▶ *the place where Jesus died.*

Add labels to your map with this information. Use your map to add further names and labels as you read the rest of this book.

2 *(a) Make a list of the different groups of people in your life (e.g. teachers, family, etc.). Then describe two occasions when these different groups might disagree and clash.*

(b) When people disagree there are a number of ways in which they react, e.g. fight – with the stronger person winning; compromise; give in; run away and avoid a fight. Describe a situation in which you have responded in one of these ways. Do you think now you reacted in the "correct" way? Explain your answer.

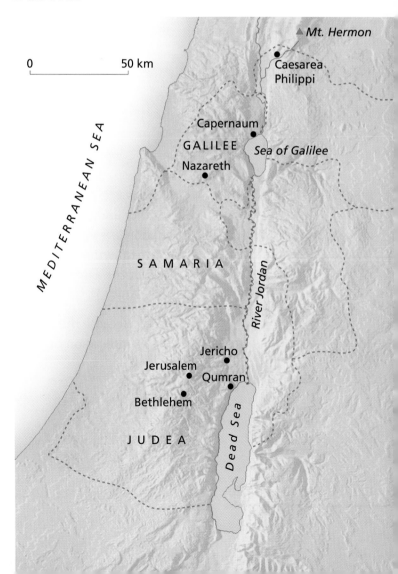

SIX

HOW DO WE KNOW ABOUT JESUS?

In this unit you are to act as private investigator. Your task is to provide reasonable evidence that Jesus existed. You uncover a number of sources of information which refer to Jesus. What did the writers think about Jesus?

Source A

Author and book:	Tacitus *The Annals of Imperial Rome*
Nationality and job:	Roman historian and senator
Date of writing:	Around 115 CE
About the extract:	Tacitus is writing about a great fire which happened in Rome in 64 CE. It was rumoured that the Emperor Nero had started this fire.

❝ To stop this rumour, Nero set up scapegoats – and punished with every refinement the notoriously depraved Christians (as they were popularly called). Christ, from whom their name comes, had been executed by the governor of Judaea, Pontius Pilate. ❞

Source B

Author and book:	Suetonius *The Twelve Caesars*
Nationality and job:	Roman historian and private secretary to Emperor Hadrian
Date of writing:	Around 119 CE
About the extract:	It is from his biography of the Emperor Claudius (ruled 41 – 54 CE).

❝ Because the Jews at Rome caused continuous disturbances at the instigation of Chrestus, Claudius expelled them from the city. ❞

 1 (a) Do you think either of these two historians gives us reasonable evidence for Jesus? Explain your opinion.

(b) Why have we so far ignored the Bible as a source of evidence?

2 Look at Source C.
Josephus was not a Christian.
Which parts of this text do you think scholars say he could not have written?

Source C

Author and book:	Josephus *The Jewish Antiquities*
Nationality and job:	Jewish; former priest and military commander in Palestine; became a Roman citizen and went to live in Rome where he wrote history books about the Jews.
Date of writing:	Around the 90s CE
Points to consider:	Most of the texts we have by Roman writers have survived because they were copied by hand by Christian scribes in the Middle Ages. They could make mistakes. They could also add to the text they were copying.

       Now there was about this time Jesus, a wise man, if it be lawful to call him a man, for he was a doer of wonderful works, a teacher of such men as receive the truth with pleasure. He won over many of the Jews, and many of the Gentiles. He was the Christ. And when Pilate, at the suggestion of the principal men among us, had condemned him to the cross, those that loved him at the beginning did not forsake him; for he appeared to them alive again at the third day; as the divine prophets had foretold, these and ten thousand other wonderful things concerning him. And the tribe of Christians, so named from him, are not extinct to this day.

Source D

Authors:	Known as Matthew, Mark, Luke and John
Name of books:	The Gospels (= "good news")
Date of writing:	Between about 60 and 100 CE
Points to consider:	The early Christians who wrote these books thought that the life, teaching and resurrection of Jesus was such good news that they wanted to tell others about it. The Gospels are sources of authority for Christians today since they are believed to contain the words of Jesus.

 3 *Each of the Gospel writers has a different style. Matthew, Mark and Luke sometimes use the same words, but there are also many differences. Rather like newspaper writers today, they were writing for different groups of people and had different sources of information. Get hold of two or three different newspapers that cover the same event. How do they differ in telling the same story? Why do they differ?*

Mary's had a baby

THE HOSTAGES ARE HOME

 4 *When you have good news you can't help but share it with somebody. Look at the headlines. What do you think are the good news stories which lie behind them?*

I got the job

THE X-RAY WAS CLEAR

SEVEN

THE BIRTH OF JESUS

In this unit you will be finding out about the Gospel stories of Jesus' birth. Was Jesus born in a stable or an inn? How many wise men visited Jesus? When was Jesus born?

Do you know?

Jesus is the Greek form of a common Jewish name: Jeshua or Joshua. It is not known in what month or year Jesus was born (possibly between 12 BCE and 4 BCE). Matthew and Luke set the place of his birth in Bethlehem perhaps because King David was born in Bethlehem, and many Jews believed the Messiah was to be a descendant of David (see Unit 4).

The story of Jesus' birth is told every Christmas when Christians come together to celebrate his birth. Christians believe that it was no ordinary birth. They believe it was the birth of God's Son. There are two accounts in the New Testament: one in Matthew's Gospel, the other in Luke. There are a number of differences. This is Luke's account:

This ninth-century Nativity cross tells the story of the events before and after Jesus' birth. The picture at the bottom shows his baptism, which you will read about in Unit 10.
Here are six captions and the reference to the relevant Gospel passage. Match the caption to the right picture.

▶ *Visitors from the east (Matthew 2:1 – 11)*

▶ *Jesus laid in a manger (Luke 2:1 – 7)*

▶ *Mary and Elizabeth (Luke 1:39 – 56)*

▶ *Jesus is presented at the Temple (Luke 2:22 – 38)*

▶ *Gabriel's message (Luke 1:26 – 38)*

▶ *The journey to Bethlehem (Luke 2:1 – 5)*

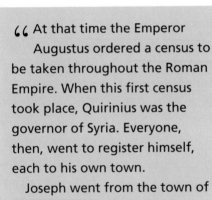

❝ At that time the Emperor Augustus ordered a census to be taken throughout the Roman Empire. When this first census took place, Quirinius was the governor of Syria. Everyone, then, went to register himself, each to his own town.

Joseph went from the town of Nazareth in Galilee to the town of Bethlehem in Judaea, the birthplace of King David. He went to register with Mary, who was pregnant, and while they were in Bethlehem, the time came for her to have her baby. She gave birth to her first son, wrapped him in strips of cloth and laid him in a manger – there was no room for them to stay in the inn. ❞
[Luke 2:1 – 7]

Luke records that shepherds visited the baby Jesus. Matthew says that wise men from the east visited him and brought gifts: gold, frankincense (a sweet-smelling tree resin) and myrrh (a bitter tree resin). Scholars think these are symbols of kingship, worship or prayer, and anointing the dead. (How many wise men were there? Read Matthew 2:1 – 12.) These symbols tell you something about Jesus.

▶ In this painting from the Philippines, what gifts are the people bringing to Jesus? Why has the painter chosen these gifts?

▶ If you were to paint a picture of the visitors to Jesus who would your visitors be and what gifts would they bring? Explain your choice.

1 ▶ Compare Matthew's account (Matthew 1:18 – 2:12) with Luke's account (Luke 2:1 – 20).
(a) What are the similarities? What are the main differences? Why do you think they differ?
(b) How does each show his belief that this was a special birth?

2 ▶ Imagine that thieves have broken into an art gallery and have stolen a picture. The only thing left is the frame with the picture title: "The Birth of God's Son". In pairs discuss what the artist might have painted. Who would be in the picture? What would people's expressions be like? What symbols might be used?

3 ▶ Write a paragraph linking the way Christmas is celebrated today with parts of the Gospel accounts (for example, think about what is often put at the top of a Christmas tree).

EIGHT

A JEWISH CHILDHOOD

The Gospels tell us that Jesus' family lived in Nazareth, a busy hillside town in Galilee. His father Joseph was a carpenter and it is likely that Jesus would have been brought up in the family firm (look up Mark 6:1 – 3). It is possible that Joseph was also a teacher of the Jewish Law, since most teachers also had a manual job at that time and we are told that Joseph was a "righteous man" (he wanted to do what God wished). Jesus' family took great care to keep the Jewish Law.

Circumcision

When he was eight days old Jesus was circumcised and named, as were all Jewish boys (Luke 2:21). Circumcision is the removal of the foreskin of a boy's penis. It was carried out in obedience to the promise made by Abraham to God (Genesis 17:10 – 14). Circumcision is a sign that a Jewish boy has become part of the people of God.

Like most Jewish boys Jesus would have attended the synagogue, his local centre of worship and education. Here he would have learnt the Jewish Scriptures. Luke's Gospel gives us another clue that Jesus was brought up to observe the Jewish Laws: "Every year the parents of Jesus went to Jerusalem for the Passover Festival" (Luke 2:41). A pilgrimage from Galilee to Jerusalem was expensive and time-consuming (it is more than 100 kilometres). They did not have to go to the Temple to celebrate – not all Jews did at the time of Jesus.

> 1 *What qualities do you think are important in parents? How do you think parents should bring up their children?*

Circumcision of Jewish boys still takes place today when the child is eight days old.

❝ When Jesus was twelve years old, they went to the festival as usual.

When the festival was over, they started back home, but the boy Jesus stayed in Jerusalem. His parents did not know this: they thought that he was with the group, so they travelled a whole day and then started looking for him among their relations and friends. They did not find him, so they went back to Jerusalem looking for him. On the third day they found him in the temple, sitting with the Jewish teachers, listening to them and asking questions. All who heard him were amazed at his intelligent answers. His parents were astonished when they saw him, and his mother said to him, "My son, why have you done this to us? Your father and I have been terribly worried trying to find you."

He answered them, "Why did you have to look for me? Didn't you know that I had to be in my Father's house?" But they did not understand his answer. ❞

[Luke 2:42 – 52]

At certain services Jewish males over the age of thirteen put leather boxes called tefillin on their forehead and left arm. These contain quotations from their Scriptures (look up Deuteronomy 6:4 – 8). Jesus may also have worn these to remind him of the commandments which every Jew must keep.

● ● ● ● ● ● ● ● ● ● ● ● ● ● ● ● ● ●

Comments on the story:

▶ At the start of each pilgrimage, pilgrims gathered in their towns and villages. As they travelled to Jerusalem groups of pilgrims would join together. It is therefore quite understandable how a self-confident child could have spent the first day of the return journey with this larger group without his parents noticing he was missing.

▶ This is the last mention of Joseph. It is possible that he died before Jesus was baptised.

2 ▶ *Who do you think Jesus was speaking of when he referred to "my Father"?*

3 ▶ *Make a list of all the things on these two pages that tell you that Jesus was Jewish.*

CALL IN THE DESERT

The Bible contains many stories of people who spent periods of time in the desert to find God in silence and prayer. In the stillness of the desert they could be alone with God. (Which group of people have you already come across in this book who sought God in the desert? Look back to Unit 4.)

1 *The photograph on this page is of the wilderness near the Dead Sea and River Jordan. Today it takes only about thirty minutes to get there by bus from Jerusalem. What words would you use to describe the scenery? What do you think it would be like to spend time here? What difficulties might you experience?*

❝ I wasn't prepared for the desert and the way it made me think and feel. It made me think about myself and what I am. There is a beautiful stillness, no noise at all, and a great feeling of space: it goes on for ever. ❞
[Anthony, aged 16]

2 *You don't have to go to the desert to feel what Anthony experienced. Is there a place where you have felt something similar? Describe it and what you felt.*

John the Baptist

In Unit 10 you will find out about an important meeting between Jesus and John the Baptist in the desert. But who was John the Baptist? Luke's Gospel says he was a cousin of Jesus (look up Luke chapter 1). The first chapter in Mark's Gospel says John appeared in the desert baptising and preaching. The Gospel writers believed that John was a prophet and that he was preparing the people for the Messiah. They believed that John was the man the prophet Isaiah was talking about when he said: "A voice cries: 'In the wilderness prepare the way of the Lord, make straight in the desert a highway for our God.'" (Isaiah 40:3). In the Bible a prophet is a person who calls people back to God.

John preached a simple message in the wilderness: Change your life – God's kingdom is here. He told people how God would punish them if they didn't change. He criticised all sin. He even criticised Herod Antipas, the ruler of Galilee in north Palestine, because he had divorced his wife to marry his brother's wife. Such a marriage was against Jewish Law.

A picture of John the Baptist. Two of the Gospel writers say that his clothes were made of camel's hair, he wore a leather belt round his waist, and ate locusts and wild honey. What did Herod Antipas do to John the Baptist? Look up Mark 6:17–29.

A modern prophet
Dietrich Bonhoeffer was a German theologian who spoke out against the Nazis when they came to power in Germany in 1933 and against their treatment of the Jews. In 1943 he plotted to overthrow Hitler. He was arrested and on 9 April 1945, a month before the end of the war in Europe, Bonhoeffer was hanged.

3 *Read Luke 3:10–14 to find out the kind of things John the Baptist told people to do to change their lives. Then imagine he has come to your school to speak about how people should change their ways today. What evils in society would he attack? What would he tell people to do?*

What do you think is going through the mind of the man who holds the placard in this photograph? What connection is there between this man and John the Baptist?

TEN

THE BAPTISM OF JESUS

Some events in life have such an effect on people that they can be called "turning-points". In this unit you will be looking at a major turning-point in Jesus' life.

1 *Have there been any major turning-points in your life? (For example, you may have been picked for a team, joined a new school, made new friends.) Write a paragraph about an event that has affected you.*

The word "baptise" comes from a Greek word meaning "to dip" in water. Water was used to show you were washing away your past sins. People came to John the Baptist to be baptised in the River Jordan. By being dipped in the water they were asking forgiveness for their past wrongdoings and showing their commitment to making a fresh start in life.

" At that time Jesus arrived from Galilee and came to John at the Jordan to be baptised by him. But John tried to make him change his mind. "I ought to be baptised by you," John said, "and yet you have come to me."

But Jesus answered him, "Let it be so for now. For in this way we shall do all that God requires." So John agreed.

As soon as Jesus was baptised, he came up out of the water. Then heaven was opened to him, and he saw the Spirit of God coming down like a dove and alighting on him. Then a voice said from heaven, "This is my own dear Son, with whom I am pleased." "
[Matthew 3:13–17]

Comments on the story:
Jesus experienced a life-changing religious experience at his baptism:
▸ He heard a voice from heaven calling him the Son of God. From now on Jesus knew that he was called by God for a special task.
▸ God's Spirit came upon him. Christians believe the Holy Spirit gives people the power to do God's will. Throughout his ministry Jesus was aware of the power of God's Spirit flowing through him.
▸ Jesus' baptism marks the beginning of his ministry – his public work.

2 *The Gospel accounts say the Holy Spirit came down on Jesus "like a dove". Some people think there was an actual dove; others think it is a way of saying that Jesus received the Spirit peacefully. Design a stained-glass window telling the story of Jesus' baptism as a turning-point in his life. If you didn't want to use a dove as a symbol for the Holy Spirit, what else could you use? What colours would you choose?*

This is a painting of Jesus' baptism by a
fifteenth-century Italian painter, Piero
della Francesca.

▶ Jot down what you can see.
▶ How has Piero painted Jesus? Why do
  you think he paints the hands in this
  way? What is the painter telling us
  about Jesus by using symbols?
▶ What do you feel about the picture?
  Do you like it? If you were to paint this
  scene, would you change anything?

This photograph shows a baptism of a
baby. Baptism is a sign that a person has
become a member of the Christian Church;
it is a practice that began very soon after
Jesus' death.

▶ What symbols can you see?
▶ Try to find out the different ways
  various Christian groups today baptise
  people (e.g. Baptists, Orthodox Church,
  Church of England). Write a report.

ELEVEN

JESUS IS TEMPTED

What things are you tempted to do? The Gospel writers record that after his baptism Jesus was tempted in the wilderness. This unit looks at what temptation is and how Jesus responded to his temptation.

1 What is temptation? How do you resist temptation? Discuss times when you think people are tempted to do something they know is wrong (e.g. shop-lifting), and what stops most people from giving way to temptation.

Some people have described temptation as a battle going on in the mind:

2 The girl in the picture has found her mother's purse lying open on the kitchen table. In pairs, write a short conversation which two halves of her mind may be having. Then read out the conversation to the rest of the class.

3 Who out of the following two people knows the power of temptation most?
Person A: Always gives in to temptation.
Person B: Resists temptation.
Explain your answer.

4 Design a poster giving practical advice on "Five ways to resist temptation".

Who is the Devil?
The Devil is also called Satan in the Bible, which comes from a Hebrew word that means "enemy". Many Christians believe in the Devil as a spiritual being who is the enemy of God. In the Bible he is pictured as a liar, a deceiver and a tempter. Artists often show the Devil as a winged creature with horns. In groups discuss what you think about the Devil.

After his baptism Jesus went into the wilderness for "forty days" – this may mean just a long period of time. He wanted to be alone to think about the special work God had called him to do. What sort of Messiah was he to be? It was here in the desert, as he was fasting, that he was tempted by the Devil.

Narrator: After spending forty days and nights without food, Jesus was hungry. Then the Devil came to him and said:

The Devil: If you are God's Son, order these stones to turn into bread.

Narrator: But Jesus answered:

Jesus: The scripture says, "Man cannot live on bread alone, but needs every word that God speaks."

Narrator: Then the Devil took Jesus to Jerusalem, the Holy City, set him on the highest point of the Temple, and said to him:

The Devil: If you are God's Son, throw yourself down, for the scriptures say, "God will give orders to his angels about you; they will hold you up with their hands, so that not even your feet will be hurt on the stones."

Jesus: But the scripture also says, "Do not put the Lord your God to the test."

Narrator: Then the Devil took Jesus to a very high mountain and showed him all the kingdoms of the world in all their greatness.

The Devil: All this I will give you, if you kneel down and worship me.

Jesus: Go away, Satan! The scripture says, "Worship the Lord your God and serve only him!"

Narrator: Then the Devil left Jesus; and the angels came and helped him.

[Matthew 4:1 – 11]

The Gospels make it clear that Jesus, like all humans, was tempted to do things he knew were wrong. But Jesus did not give in to temptation.

5 *Match up Jesus' temptations with this list.*
(a) To be the greatest king on earth.
(b) To use his power to impress people.
(c) To use magical powers to help himself and others on earth with material things like food.

6 *Imagine you are a book illustrator. You have been asked to illustrate the story of Jesus' temptations. How would you draw your illustration to bring out the theme of temptation? Sketch it if you like.*

This is a painting by Stanley Spencer called Christ in the Wilderness: Rising from Sleep in the Morning. *It was painted in 1940. Spencer tried to imagine what happened to Jesus in the wilderness and felt he was in a wilderness himself. He wrote about this time in his life: "it was God and me all the time".*

▶ *What do you think Spencer is saying about Jesus' time in the wilderness in this picture? Is Jesus finding it easy to resist temptation?*

TWELVE

MAN WITH A MISSION

"Our mission is to boldly go where no man has gone before..." These famous words of Captain Kirk as he treks through space sound very exciting. Do you have your own personal mission in life? In this unit you will find out about the mission which Jesus felt called to.

After his temptations Jesus went back to Galilee. One day in Nazareth he was asked to read the Scripture in the synagogue. He read this from Isaiah:

> 66 "The Spirit of the Lord is upon me,
> because he has chosen me to bring good news to the poor.
> He has sent me to proclaim liberty to the captives
> and recovery of sight to the blind;
> to set free the oppressed
> and announce that the time has come when the Lord will save his people."
> Jesus rolled up the scroll, gave it back to the attendant, and sat down. All the people in the synagogue had their eyes fixed on him, as he said to them, "This passage of scripture has come true today, as you heard it being read." 99
>
> [Luke 4:18–21]

Comments on the story:
- This is what the prophet Isaiah believed the Messiah would do.
- Jesus used the quotation to sum up what his work was to be. He was saying that he was the Messiah.

A mission to outsiders

"Outsiders" are people who do not fit into a group. They often feel left out. They may be prisoners, people who take drugs, people who are ill or disabled, people who are poor.

Jesus made it clear that he came for outsiders. Luke's Gospel (Luke 19:1 – 10) tells of the meeting between a tax collector called Zacchaeus and Jesus. Because tax collectors collected money for the Romans they were disliked by their fellow Jews. The story is shown on the page opposite.

 1 (a) Have you ever felt like an outsider? In groups share what it feels like. Why do friends sometimes make others feel like outsiders?
(b) List different groups of people in our society who are often treated as outsiders. Try to explain why they are treated like that.

 2 Imagine that you were Zacchaeus, or one of the outcasts in Luke 5:12 – 14 or Luke 7:36 – 50. Write a diary account of your meeting with Jesus. Record your feelings before and after the meeting.

Narrator: *Jesus went on into Jericho and was passing through. There was a chief tax collector there named Zacchaeus, who was rich. He was trying to see who Jesus was, but he was a little man and could not see Jesus because of the crowd.*

So he ran ahead of the crowd and climbed a sycamore tree to see Jesus, who was going to pass that way. When Jesus came to that place, he looked up.
Jesus: *Hurry down, Zacchaeus, because I must stay in your house today.*

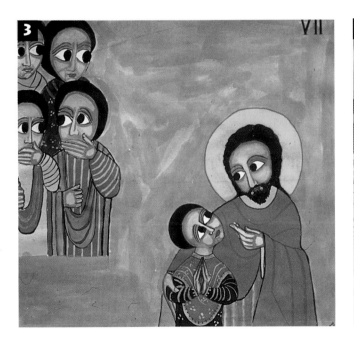

Narrator: *Zacchaeus hurried down and welcomed him with great joy. All the people who saw it started grumbling:*
Grumbling person: *This man has gone as a guest to the home of a sinner!*

Narrator: *Zacchaeus stood up and said to the Lord:*
Zacchaeus: *Listen, sir! I will give half my belongings to the poor, and if I have cheated anyone, I will pay him back four times as much.*
Jesus: *Salvation has come to this house today … The Son of Man came to seek and to save the lost.*

FOLLOW ME!

Jesus' ministry began around the Sea of Galilee. The town of Capernaum became his base. (Look back at the map on p.13.) Like many "rabbis" at the time (respected Jewish teachers), some men became his disciples (pupils). They often called Jesus "Rabbi" or "Teacher". Luke records that there was a main group of about seventy disciples. Out of these Jesus chose twelve to be his "apostles". The word means "people who are sent out". They were to go out and carry on his work. They were a mixed bunch of people: fishermen, a tax collector, a revolutionary. They were ordinary men – not particularly good or religious.

He told the twelve, "I have chosen you to be with me. I will also send you out to preach, and you will have authority to drive out demons."

(Mark 3:14 – 15). This is Mark's list of the twelve: Simon (Jesus gave him the name Peter), James and his brother John (sons of Zebedee), Andrew, Philip, Bartholomew, Matthew, Thomas, James, Thaddaeus, Simon the Patriot (or Zealot), and Judas Iscariot.

Being a disciple was a costly business. Jesus made it clear that it was not like a hobby. Instead it was a life-time commitment. It meant:
▶ leaving home, family and friends
▶ travelling the country (on foot)
▶ total commitment.

▶ *What do you think is important to these people? What do you think their lives are like?*

▶ *Jesus said having money made it difficult for a person to enter the Kingdom of God. What temptations might a person have who has a lot of money?*

Jesus said: "None of you can be my disciple unless he gives up every thing he has." (Luke 14:33). When Jesus called people to follow him it was to a complete change of life. Not all found this easy. A rich young man asked Jesus what he must do to receive eternal life and said he obeyed all the commandments:

> ❝ Jesus looked straight at him with love and said, "You need only one thing. Go and sell all you have and give the money to the poor, and you will have riches in heaven; then come and follow me." When the man heard this, gloom spread over his face, and he went away sad, because he was very rich.
>
> Jesus looked round at his disciples and said to them, "How hard it will be for rich people to enter the Kingdom of God!" ❞
> [Mark 10:21–23]

1 ▶ Use library books to find out what happened, or what legends say happened, to the following disciples after Jesus' death: Peter, James son of Zebedee (sometimes called James the Great), Andrew, Thomas. (You will find out more about Judas in Unit 25.)

2 ▶ What four things would you find hardest to give up in life to follow someone? Explain why.

16 November 1989

SIX PRIESTS MURDERED IN EL SALVADOR

Today six priests were shot dead. It is believed that the murders were the work of government officials. The priests had dared to criticise the rulers about their treatment of the poor. In the manner of Jesus, they spoke out against poverty, homelessness and the denial of human rights.

Jesus called his disciples to love others by serving them. Today Christians throughout the world put this love into practice in many different ways (look at Unit 29). Jesus warned his disciples that following him would at times be a dangerous business: "I am sending you out just like sheep to a pack of wolves … Watch out, for there will be men who will arrest you and take you to court … Everyone will hate you because of me." (Matthew 10:16 – 22). Even today Jesus' followers are persecuted in parts of the world.

When Jesus chose his first disciples he called them to go out and preach the Gospel (the "good news") which he had come to give. Christians have always thought it important to tell others about Jesus.

Do you think this picture shows a good way of "spreading the good news"?

3 ▶ A person needed to show great commitment to be a disciple.
   (a) What things in your life do you need to show commitment to? (e.g. To be good at sport you need to train hard.)
   (b) How can showing commitment be a costly experience? (e.g. How can training to be a good sports player be costly?)

4 ▶ Design a poster called "Follow Me" that a church might display outside on its notice board.

FOURTEEN

THE RABBI OF NAZARETH

In this unit you will learn about Jesus as a teacher and his teaching about prayer.

 1 *Which qualities do you think are the most important in order to be a good teacher?*

Jesus was called "rabbi" by his followers. It means "teacher". Jesus was such a popular teacher that on occasions he was nearly mobbed by crowds who had come to hear him. He was often invited into people's homes to interpret the Scriptures. Mark says that once when he taught in the synagogue at Capernaum, "The people who heard him were amazed at the way he taught, for he wasn't like the teachers of the Law; instead he taught with authority." (Mark 1:22). When Jesus was asked where he got his authority from, he replied: "What I teach is not my own teaching, but it comes from God, who sent me." (John 7:16).

Not everyone liked his teachings – he was not afraid to criticise people when they were wrong. Like many Jewish teachers of the time, Jesus often used parables to communicate with his listeners. These can be quite short sayings or even long stories, which use everyday events or objects to put across a deeper message. For example, instead of just saying, "Be humble when you pray", Jesus told a story about a Pharisee and a tax collector. (Look it up in Luke 18:9 – 14.)

Prayer

Jesus regularly went away from the crowds to be alone with God. Matthew and Luke say he taught his disciples how to pray by giving them a model prayer in which he taught them to address God as "Abba" (Father). It is the basis of the Lord's Prayer said today by Christians.

Prayer has been described as "wasting time with God". It's like being in any other loving relationship. When you love someone deeply you want to talk to them and tell them everything. At other times you just want to be with them, not saying anything. You just like being with the other person. One teenager said, "At times I remain silent. Prayer gives me time to stop and be still and think about what I am doing with my life."

The Lord's Prayer

Our Father in heaven,
may your name be honoured,
may your kingdom come,
may your will be done,
on earth as it is in heaven.
Give us today the food we need.
Forgive us our sins
as we forgive the wrongs that others have done to us.
Do not bring us to hard testing,
but keep us safe from the evil one.

[Matthew 6:9 – 13]

How can you tell that this person is praying? What might she be praying about? What feelings do you associate with this photograph? What questions would you want to ask her?

This is another parable Jesus told about prayer (Luke 18: 1 – 8):

 2 (a) Put Jesus' teaching about prayer into one sentence.
   (b) Which kind of teaching do you think might have more impact: Jesus' parable or your sentence? Why?

 3 (a) What do you think the person meant when he said prayer is like "wasting time with God"?
   (b) Why do you think that Jesus thought it was important to spend so much time in prayer? Do you take time out to be silent and think about what you are doing in life? If you do, try to explain why.

FIFTEEN

THE SERMON ON THE MOUNT

In this unit you will be exploring what attitudes and values are important to make a person happy. You will also learn what Jesus taught about happiness and how to behave towards others.

Happiness is . . . ?

1 *Look at this picture. In pairs discuss what would make you happy. Would you include any of the things in the picture? Feed back your ideas to the class.*

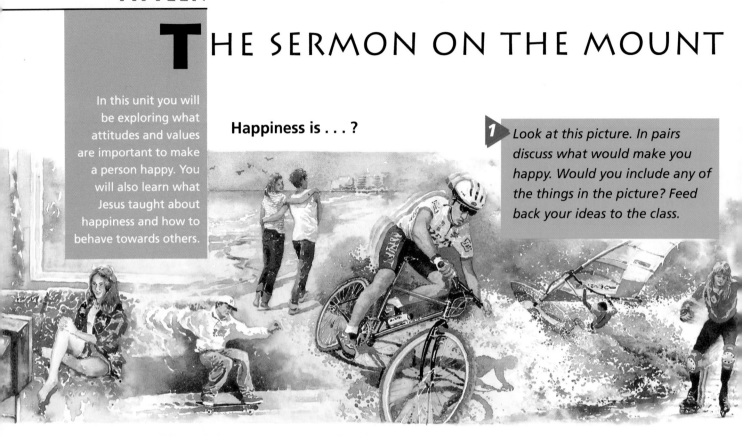

2 *Many people believe that happiness can be created by having money. Why do a lot of people play the National Lottery? If you won the jackpot prize, what would you do with the money? In December 1994 a man won £18 million on the lottery. This is how one newspaper reported the effects which it had upon him:*

The family of the dad who scooped the £18 million lottery jackpot begged him to give it back today. He has told relatives, "This has made my life a nightmare."

Why do you think winning the lottery made this man's life a nightmare?

One day Jesus went up a hill and talked to his followers about happiness. He said the following people were happy (or "blessed"):

Happy are . . .

    those who know their need of God

    those who mourn

    those who are humble

    those whose greatest desire is to do what
       God requires

    those who are merciful to others

    the pure in heart

    those who work for peace

    those who are persecuted because they do
    what God requires. (Matthew 5:3 – 10)

Jesus turned the values which people often have upside down. He did not link happiness with ambition, fame and money. Instead, he said it was to do with what sort of person you are. He taught that the truly happy people are the ones who base their lives upon God and know they need God.

3 ▸ *Match up these two photographs with two of the categories of people Jesus said were happy.*

The United Nations peace-keeping force in Bosnia

Mother Teresa caring for a baby

4 ▸ *Take each of the people whom Jesus said were happy and give its opposite. For example, what could "the proud" be the opposite of?*

How to treat others

The teachings that Jesus gave on the hill are known as the Sermon on the Mount. In addition to teaching about happiness, the Sermon on the Mount also contains teaching about how people should treat each other. "Whatever you wish that men would do to you, do so to them." (Matthew 7:12). This has been called the "Golden Rule". One version of the Bible translated it as: "Here is a simple rule of thumb for behaviour. Ask yourself what you want people to do for you. Then seize the opportunity to do it for them first. Giving, not getting, is the way."

"You have heard that people were told in the past, 'Do not commit murder; anyone who does will be brought to trial.' But now I tell you: whoever is angry with his brother will be brought to trial." (Matthew 5:21 – 22)

6 ▸ *(a) Name three things which make you angry.*
(b) When someone makes you angry do you:
▸ *lash out in retaliation*
▸ *hold a grudge and refuse to speak to the person*
▸ *calmly talk the issue through*
▸ *think seriously about whether you have done something which has caused them to be angry?*
(c) Which do you think is the best response? Say why.

5 ▸ *Do you agree? Does giving and not getting make a person happy?*

33

SIXTEEN

"GOD RULES OK!"

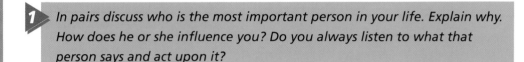

Who do you listen to when you are trying to make decisions in life: a parent, friend, teacher? In this unit you will be thinking about the influences on your life, and learning what Jesus taught to be the most important influence.

1 *In pairs discuss who is the most important person in your life. Explain why. How does he or she influence you? Do you always listen to what that person says and act upon it?*

Jesus summed up his teaching in the following words: "The right time has come and the Kingdom of God is near! Turn away from your sins and believe the Good News!" (Mark 1:15). By using the phrase "Kingdom of God" Jesus did not mean a place. Instead, he was referring to the rule of God. Jesus called people to accept God as their King and to put God at the centre of their lives. His message could be summed up as "God Rules OK!"

Jesus taught that God was working through him in a special way. God's rule was being shown both by his teaching and by his miracles (Luke 11:20). He taught that the most important thing in life was to do what God wills. Everything else was of secondary importance.

Jesus used examples from everyday life to explain about the kingdom.

"The Kingdom of heaven is like this. A man happens to find a treasure hidden in a field. He covers it up again, and is so happy that he goes and sells everything he has, and then goes back and buys that field." (Matthew 13:44)

Many of Jesus' parables were about the Kingdom of God. In some, Jesus taught that the kingdom was present already in the lives of those people who had accepted God's rule. He said, "the Kingdom of God is within you". In other parables Jesus taught that not everyone yet accepted God as their king. The Kingdom of God would come in completeness only in the future. He told one parable about wheat and weeds (Matthew 13:24–30). Look at page 35.

2 *What do you think is the most important thing in life? Put these words in order of importance: the first one, the most important; the last one, the least important:*

- good looks
- family
- good health
- a reason for living
- fame

- money
- believing in God
- a high IQ
- love
- popularity

The Kingdom of Heaven is like this. A man sowed good seed in his field. One night, when everyone was asleep, an enemy came and sowed weeds among the wheat and went away.

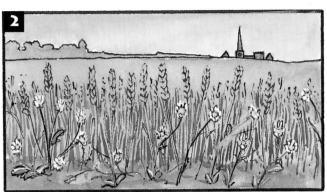

When the plants grew and the ears of corn began to form, then the weeds showed up.

The man's servants came to him and said...
"Sir, it was good seed you sowed in your field; where did the weeds come from?"
"It was some enemy who did this," he answered.

"Do you want us to go and pull up the weeds?" they asked him.
"No," he answered, "because as you gather the weeds you might pull up some of the wheat along with them."

"Let the wheat and the weeds grow together until harvest. Then I will tell the harvest workers to pull up the weeds first, tie them in bundles and burn them . . .

. . . and then to gather in the wheat and put it in my barn."

 In the Bible the harvest is a common symbol for God's judgement. So what do you think we can learn from this story?

 Imagine someone has decided to put God at the centre of his or her life. Would that life be different? If so, in what ways?

SEVENTEEN

HO IS MY NEIGHBOUR?

In this and the next unit you will explore two of Jesus' best-known parables. Here you will find out his answer to the question "What kind of people should I help?"

The Good Samaritan (Luke 10:25 – 37)

A teacher of the Law came up to Jesus and asked, "How do I get eternal life?" Jesus asked him what the Scriptures said. The man answered, "Love God with all your heart and love your neighbour as you love yourself." Jesus said he was right. But the man asked Jesus, "Who is my neighbour?" And Jesus told this story:

There was once a man who was going down from Jerusalem to Jericho when robbers attacked him, stripped him, and beat him up, leaving him half dead.

A priest was going down that road; but when he saw the man, he walked on by, on the other side.

A Levite also came along, went over and looked at the man, and then walked on by, on the other side.

But when a Samaritan saw him his heart was filled with pity.

Who's who?

Samaritans

These were people who lived in Samaria, in Palestine. They worshipped the same God as the Jews, but the Jews and the Samaritans hated each other.

The priest and the Levite

These were Jewish religious leaders who were expected to keep the Law of God. The Law demanded that they love their neighbours. They believed this to mean their Jewish neighbours.

He went over to him, poured oil and wine on his wounds and bandaged them.

Then he put the man on his own animal and took him to an inn, where he took care of him.

The next day he took out two silver coins and gave them to the innkeeper . . .

"Take care of him, and when I come back this way, I will pay you whatever else you spend on him."

Jesus concluded . . .
"Which one of these three acted like a neighbour towards the man attacked by the robbers?"

1 (a) What answer would you have given Jesus?
(b) What answer did the teacher of the Law give to Jesus? Look it up in Luke 10:37.

2 With a partner work out what a "good Samaritan" might do today if he or she came across the following:
(a) a tramp sleeping rough in a shop doorway
(b) thugs attacking an old man.
Then discuss your suggestions in class.

3 In groups design a collage with the title "Who is my neighbour?" Cut pictures out of magazines and newspapers of people who are in need of help. Add labels saying what kind of help they might need. Suggest who is responsible for dealing with the situations you have selected.

EIGHTEEN

Forgiveness

Do you find it easy to forgive people or say sorry? In this unit you will learn what Jesus taught about forgiveness.

Jesus taught his followers a lot about forgiveness. He told the following story about a father and his two sons (Luke 15:11 – 32). It was a story to help people understand the nature of God's love. It is often known as the parable of the Prodigal Son.

The Prodigal Son

Once a man had two sons. The younger said to him, "Give me my share of the property now."

The son sold the property and left home with the money. He spent it all on wild living.

Then he had to find work and was given a job looking after pigs. No one gave him anything to eat. At last he came to his senses . . .

"All my father's hired workers have more than they can eat, and here I am about to starve!"

He decided to go home and say sorry to his father and ask for a job as one of his hired workers. He was still a long way from home when his father saw him and ran to meet him.

"Father, I have sinned against God and against you. I am no longer fit to be called your son."

But the father called his servants. "Let us celebrate with a feast!"

The elder son heard the sound of feasting. He asked a servant . . . "What's going on?" "Your brother has come home."

The elder brother was so angry he wouldn't go into the house. He told his father. "Look, all these years I have worked for you like a slave. What have you given me? Not even a goat for me to have a feast with my friends!"

"My son, you are always here with me, and everything I have is yours. But we had to celebrate and be happy, because your brother was dead, but now he is alive; he was lost, but now he has been found."

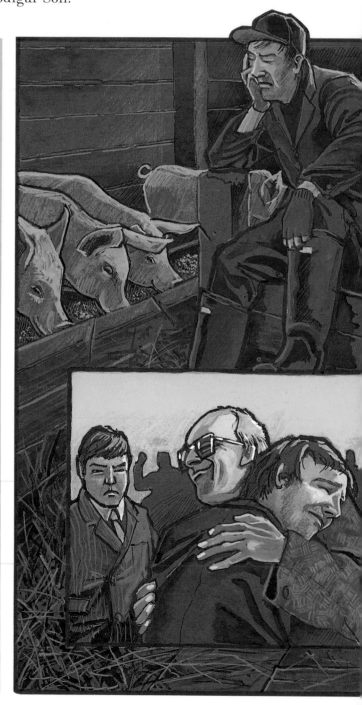

1 *The Prodigal Son said sorry. Do you ever find it difficult to say sorry? If so why?*

2 *Who stands for God in the story? What do the two sons stand for?*

3 *Imagine the meeting between the two brothers. What do you think they say to each other? Is the elder brother still angry? Does he eventually welcome his brother home? Work on a short scene between them with a partner. You could then role-play it to the rest of the class.*

16-YEAR-OLD GIRL MISSING AFTER FIGHT WITH MUM

14-year-old runs away from home after row with parents

4 *(a) What reasons might teenagers have for wanting to leave home?*
(b) What might parents feel when their children run away? What do you think the father in the story felt? How can you tell?

Is it always right to forgive?

SIX-YEAR-OLD DEAD
Parents forgive drunk driver

A clergyman and his wife have forgiven the drunk driver who killed their son. The father said:

"We had to forgive the driver because every day we say the Lord's Prayer and we would choke on it if we were not forgiving. I know that God has had to forgive me a whole lot of things and I couldn't receive God's forgiveness if I couldn't forgive others who have sinned.

"You have to find a way of hating the sin and loving the sinner.

"When we bottle up anger we destroy ourselves by the failure to forgive. Forgiveness is not an optional extra - we have to do it. Forgiveness is a form of love."

5 *Jesus taught his disciples that they must forgive "seventy times seven" (Matthew 18:22). He meant "always". Read the article about the drunk driver and in groups have a discussion: Is it always right or possible to forgive? Are there any situations where you think it would be wrong to forgive?*

Jesus taught people to pray:

▶ "Forgive us the wrongs we have done, as we forgive the wrongs that others have done to us." (Matthew 6:12)

Jesus also taught:
▶ Love your enemies and pray for those who persecute you." (Matthew 5:44)

On the cross Jesus cried out:
▶ "Forgive them, Father! They don't know what they are doing." (Luke 23:34)

ORKER OF MIRACLES

1 *In your opinion, do any of the pictures on this page show a miracle? Discuss what you think a miracle is. Then come up with a group definition.*

The Gospel writers record about thirty-five miracles that Jesus performed. The writers believed that miracles showed the power of God at work.

Today people have different opinions about the miracles.

▶ "It's not important whether they happened; what's important is what they mean."

▶ "In those days people didn't understand about science and nature as we do; one day science will be able to explain all his miracles."

▶ "God created the laws of nature. He can therefore act in nature for special reasons."

Jesus' miracles can be divided into four groups.

Group 1: Nature miracles

There are a number of occasions in the Gospels when Jesus shows God's power over nature: he calms a storm on the Sea of Galilee (Mark 4:35–41), he turns water into wine at a wedding (John 2:1–11). One miracle occurs in all four Gospel accounts. It is the account of how Jesus fed 5000 people from five loaves and two fish. Read it for yourself in Luke 9:12–17.

Miracle on the runway

A Boeing 747 with 254 passengers on board lies on the runway after crashing...... but miraculously no one was injured

Comments on the story in Luke 9: 12–17.

▸ The Jews believed that when the Messiah came he would feed the hungry in the same way that God had fed them when they escaped from Egypt and wandered in the wilderness.

▸ The Gospel writers believed that this miracle showed that Jesus was acting by God's power. He was bringing in God's rule in his own actions.

belief that Jesus is victor over the many powers that can destroy a person's life:

> Jesus is the conqueror;
> he overcame magic,
> he overcame amulets and charms,
> he overcame the darkness of demon possession,
> he overcame dread.
> When we are with him,
> we also conquer.
>
> *(African Christian song from the Transvaal)*

2 *Some Christians think that Jesus did actually multiply the food. Others think that it was a miracle of sharing. That is, Jesus stopped people being selfish and taught them to share the food they had with others. Would it be a "miracle" for the world to learn to share today? Imagine that one day the whole world has decided to share the earth's resources. Write a news article about this.*

Group 2: Exorcisms

Jesus is often shown as struggling with evil powers (look back at Unit 11). The Gospels also record a number of times during his ministry when Jesus cast evil spirits out of people. We call these "exorcisms".

In Africa today Jesus is most commonly called the Victor. Here is a song that expresses this

3 *What do you think of the African picture of Jesus below? How does it differ from other pictures you have seen? How would you represent a "victor" over fear or sickness in your world?*

4 *Look up one of the following exorcisms Jesus performed: in Matthew 12 : 22 – 32 or Mark 5 : 1 – 20.*
(a) Explain what happened.
(b) How did people react to what Jesus did? Why do you think they reacted in this way?

5 *Sometimes people today talk about other people being "possessed", or taken over, by modern-day demons, e.g. drugs. In pairs make a list of modern-day demons. What power do they have over people? How do people get released from them?*

An African picture of Jesus casting out an evil spirit (read Mark 9 : 14 – 29).

TWENTY

ESUS THE HEALER

This unit continues to look at the miracles of Jesus. What would be the *ultimate* miracle that anybody could perform?

Group 3: Raising of the dead

The Gospels record three occasions in which Jesus raised people back from the dead:

▶ Jairus' twelve-year-old daughter (for example, Mark 5:21 – 24, 35 – 43)
▶ a widow's son at Nain (Luke 7:11 – 17)
▶ Lazarus, a friend of Jesus (John 11:1 – 44).

In his gospel, John does not use the word "miracle". Instead he talks about "signs". Just as a road sign points to something, so the miracles are signs that point to Jesus. They tell the reader something about who Jesus was, about his special relationship with God, and about the coming of the Kingdom of God.

 Read the account of the raising of Lazarus in the Bible. Imagine that you are a reporter sent by a local newspaper or radio station to interview an eyewitness. Ask him or her to describe what happened from their point of view. What did they hear, see, feel? What did this incident tell them about Jesus? Then write your article, giving your opinion about what the eyewitness said.

When you have read the page opposite look at this cloth from Ethiopia. Which two kinds of healing does it show? John the Baptist sent two of his followers to Jesus to ask: "Are you he who is to come?" What did Jesus answer? Look up Luke 7:22 – 23.

Group 4: Healing miracles

We have already seen that Jesus described his mission as giving recovery of sight to the blind and setting captives free (look back to Unit 12). Jesus understood his miracles to be the way of announcing "that the time has come when the Lord will save his people" (Luke 4:19). Part of the mission was to set free the outcasts, to make them feel loved. At other times he showed God's healing power.

Leprosy is a skin disease that is still found today in Africa and Asia. Numb blotches on the skin appear which can spread and lead to the sufferer becoming deformed, crippled or paralysed. It used to be thought that it could be caught easily just by touching someone. Lepers lived away from other people to prevent the spreading of the disease. They had to cry "Unclean! Unclean!" so other people knew not to come near.

> **Narrator:** A man suffering from leprosy came to Jesus, knelt down, and begged him for help.
> **Man:** If you want to, you can make me clean.
> **Narrator:** Jesus was filled with pity, and stretched out his hand and touched him.
> **Jesus:** I do want to. Be clean!
> **Narrator:** At once the disease left the man, and he was clean. Then Jesus spoke sternly to him.
> **Jesus:** Listen, don't tell anyone about this.
> [Mark 1:40–44]

Today the Church continues Jesus' healing work, mainly through Christians being involved in medical treatment and research. There is also a ministry of healing: one church in three in England now has healing services. The fastest growing churches in America are the Charismatic and Pentecostal churches where worship is centred around "signs and wonders", including miracles of healing. Not all Christians experience physical healing when they pray for it, but some believe they do. Look at this newspaper report:

> In 1986 Julie Sheldon was struck down by an illness called dystonia which caused her body to go into violent and uncontrollable spasms. Doctors told her that there was no cure. She recalls: "Four or five times a day my head would be sent crashing back – so far that it felt as if I was being throttled."
> The next three years were spent in and out of hospital. In 1989 her friends thought she was dying. Then Jim Glennon, a priest with a healing ministry, came to pray for her. From that day on she started to get gradually better. Now her doctors talk of a miracle.
>
> (Daily Mail, 23 January 1995)

2 *Jesus was not afraid to touch the leper. What does this tell you about Jesus?*

3 *Find out about the healing miracles which Christians believe take place at Lourdes in France. Write up your findings including your own opinions.*

4 *Was it a miracle? Or a coincidence? Or is there another explanation? Discuss what you think.*

5 *In a poll carried out by Time magazine in April 1995, 69 per cent of Americans said they believed in miracles. Carry out your own survey. Plot your findings in the form of a chart.*

TWENTY-ONE

THE TRANSFIGURATION

What do other people think about you? Do their opinions matter? In this unit you will be learning about how other people saw Jesus and how Jesus changed their understanding of who he was.

1 *In groups of five choose one person for the others in the group to write about. The other four people write a short description of the person, including physical details as well as a character description. When you have finished read out the descriptions. How are they the same? How do they differ? Why do you think they differ?*

One day Jesus took his disciples to the area around Caesarea Philippi (look back at the map on page 13). On the way he asked them:

Jesus: Tell me, who do people say I am?
Disciple: Some say you are John the Baptist; others say that you are Elijah, while others say that you are one of the prophets.
Jesus: What about you? Who do you say I am?

Narrator: Peter answered:
Peter: You are the Messiah.
Narrator: Then Jesus ordered them:
Jesus: Do not tell anyone about me.
[Mark 8:27–30]

Why did Jesus order his disciples to keep silent? Jesus was worried that people would have a wrong understanding of who he was. You may remember from Unit 4 that at that time many Jews thought that God would send a Messiah who would be a military leader to overthrow Roman rule. Jesus went on to teach his disciples that he was not that sort of leader. What he said came as a shock to them:

Narrator: Jesus began to teach his disciples:
Jesus: The Son of Man must suffer much and be rejected by the elders, the chief priests, and the teachers of the Law. He will be put to death, but three days later he will rise to life.

Peter: This shall not happen to you. It must never happen!
Jesus: Your thoughts do not come from God but from man! It is God's will that I must die and rise again.
[Mark 8:31–33]

2 *Why do you think Peter reacted in the way he did?*

A few days later some of the disciples had an amazing experience which confirmed in their minds that Jesus was the Messiah, God's special chosen one who had been sent to save them:

Six days later Jesus took with him Peter, James and John, and led them up a high mountain, where they were alone. As they looked on a change came over Jesus and his clothes became shining white – whiter than anyone in the world could wash them. Then the three disciples saw Elijah and Moses talking with Jesus. Peter spoke up and said to Jesus, "Teacher, how good it is that we are here! We will make three tents, one for you, one for Moses and one for Elijah." He and the others were so frightened that he did not know what to say.

Then a cloud appeared and covered them with its shadow, and a voice came from the cloud, "This is my own dear Son – listen to him!" They took a quick look round but did not see anyone else; only Jesus was with them.

As they came down the mountain, Jesus ordered them, "Don't tell anyone what you have seen, until the Son of Man has risen from death."
[Mark 9:2 – 9]

Who's who?

Moses
Moses represents the Law. He rescued the Jews from slavery in Egypt and led them towards the Promised Land of Israel. In the book of Exodus in the Old Testament you can read how God appeared to Moses on Mount Sinai and gave him the Law (which included the Ten Commandments). The Jews expected someone like Moses to return at the time of the Messiah (Deuteronomy 18:18).

Elijah
Elijah represents the prophets. He was a prophet of the ninth century BCE. In the book of Kings in the Old Testament we read that God appeared to him on Mount Horeb (1 Kings 19:8 – 13). The Jews expected Elijah to return when the Messiah came (Malachi 4:5).

3 Imagine that you were one of the disciples present at this event. Write a short account, or give a radio interview, of what you saw and heard. Include the feelings you had. Whose did you think was the voice "from the cloud"?

4 Read the account of the meeting between God and Moses in Exodus 24: 15 – 18 and 34:29 – 30. List three similarities between this story and the Transfiguration.

This event is called the Transfiguration – a word that refers to the changed appearance of Jesus.
▶ Who are the two men with Jesus in this stained-glass window?
▶ What might their appearance with Jesus have meant to the three disciples watching?

TWENTY-TWO

JESUS' TEACHING ABOUT HIMSELF

Everyone who met Jesus could see that he was someone special. In this unit you will be finding out what Jesus taught about himself.

Jesus often spoke of a special relationship he had with God. He calls him "Father" and himself the "Son". (For example, look up Matthew 11:27). According to John's Gospel he identified himself with God and told his followers that "The Father and I are one."

> **About John's Gospel**
> This has many differences from the other Gospels – those of Matthew, Mark and Luke. Most people think it was written later than the others because the writer is less interested in Jesus as a human being and more interested in him as the Son of God. Some scholars think that John used material that the other Gospel writers didn't know about.

I am

In John's Gospel Jesus uses seven sayings to describe himself. They all start with the words "I am".

1 Here are some things in John's Gospel that Jesus said about himself.
Match each statement with its reference:
- "I have come down from heaven."
- "What I teach is not my own teaching, but it comes from God, who sent me."
- "The Father and I are one."
- "Whoever has seen me has seen the Father."
(a) John 10:30
(b) John 6:38
(c) John 7:16
(d) John 14:9

1 *"I am the bread of life. He who comes to me will never be hungry; he who believes in me will never be thirsty."* (John 6:35)

One of the miracles Jesus performed was to feed 5000 people with a few loaves and fish – look back to Unit 19. But Jesus taught that he came to give more than physical food for the stomach. This photograph shows a Roman Catholic priest holding up the wafer – the bread. The priest has said, "It will become for us the bread of life."

2 *"I am the light of the world. Whoever follows me will have the light of life and will never walk in darkness."* (John 8:12)

3 *"I am the gate for the sheep . . . Whoever comes in by me will be saved."* (John 10:7, 9)

4 *"I am the good shepherd, who is willing to die for the sheep."* (John 10:11)

In Jesus' day shepherds cared for their sheep day and night, finding them pasture and protecting them from danger. This modern shepherd in the Middle East does much the same 2000 years later.

5 *"I am the resurrection and the life. Whoever believes in me will live, even though he dies; and whoever lives and believes in me will never die."* (John 11:25 – 6) (Jesus said this just before he raised Lazarus from the dead: look back to Unit 20.)

6 *"I am the way, the truth, and the life: no one goes to the Father except by me."* (John 14:6)

7 *"I am the real vine, and my Father is the gardener."* (John 15:1)

2 ▶ Design a banner or wall hanging for a Christian using all of these sayings, but without using words.

3 ▶ Read the account of Moses' meeting with God in Exodus chapter 3. How does God appear to Moses? What name does God use of himself? What connections are there between God's name and the titles Jesus uses in John's Gospel?

TWENTY-THREE

CONFLICT

In this unit you will be considering the causes of conflict in today's society and examining why Jesus came into conflict with the religious authorities.

▶ *What is happening in this photograph? What might have caused this situation to occur? Give the photograph a newspaper headline.*

1 *Look through a newspaper. List or cut out conflicts:*
- *between individual people*
- *between people and the government*
- *between nations.*

Conflict often happens because of a clash of opinions. When people feel threatened they sometimes fight back. During his ministry Jesus had attacked wrongdoing at all levels – even among the religious authorities. During the last week of his life the religious authorities (who felt threatened by Jesus) hit back. They managed to get Jesus killed.

Jesus enters Jerusalem

The week started when Jesus entered Jerusalem for the festival of Passover. We are told that as Jesus entered the city he was greeted with the words: "Praise God! God bless him who comes in the name of the Lord!" This was a familiar way of greeting visitors to the holy city at festival time.

Christians today celebrate Jesus' entry into Jerusalem on Palm Sunday. They walk in processions and carry palm crosses.

Jesus in the Temple

During the last week Jesus taught in the Temple daily and greatly upset the chief priests and the Temple authorities, for three reasons:

1 He predicted the end of the chief priests:

> 66 Jesus told this parable: "A man planted a vineyard, let it out to tenants and went abroad. Later he sent a slave for his share of the harvest but the tenants beat the slave. So he sent another slave, but the tenants beat him also. Then he sent a third slave; the tenants wounded him too. Finally, the owner sent his son. But when the tenants saw him they said 'This is the owner's son. Let's kill him, and his property will be ours!' So they killed him. What then will the owner do? He will come and kill those men, and hand the vineyard over to other tenants." 99
>
> [based on Luke 20:9–16]

● ·

Comments on the story
- The vineyard was the Jewish nation.
- The tenants were the Temple authorities and chief priests.
- Who was the owner? Who was the son? Who do you think were the slaves?

2 He showed his opposition to the chief priests in what he did:

> 66 Then Jesus went into the Temple and began to drive out the merchants, saying to them, "It is written in the Scriptures that God said, 'My Temple will be called a house of prayer.' But you have turned it into a hideout for thieves!" 99
>
> [Luke 19:45–46]

3 He predicted the destruction of the Temple. Some of the disciples were talking about the Temple, how beautiful it looked with its fine stones and the gifts offered to God. Jesus said, "All this you see – the time will come when not a single stone here will be left in its place: every one will be thrown down." (Luke 21:5-6).

2 *How did the Temple authorities and chief priests react to Jesus' parable? Look up Luke 20:19–20.*

3 *What is it like to feel threatened? What forms can threatening take? How do different people react to being threatened? Which do you think is the best reaction? Explain why.*

Jews from all over the Roman Empire came to the Temple to worship. They needed to change their money into local coins to buy a sacrifice for the Temple and also to pay the Temple tax. The Temple authorities made a massive profit from this trade.
This famous painting by El Greco (1541 – 1614) is called "Christ Driving the Money-changers from the Temple."

TWENTY-FOUR

THE LAST SUPPER

In this unit you will be finding out about the special meal that Jesus had with his disciples the night before he died, and how Jesus spent his last hours before he was arrested. You will also find out how Christians celebrate this last meal today.

Passover

Many people think that Jesus' last meal with his disciples was a Passover meal. Passover is a festival in the spring still held by Jews today. It celebrates the time when God freed the Jews from slavery in Egypt, over 3000 years ago.

Jerusalem was crowded at Passover time because Jews came from all over Palestine to celebrate the festival at the Temple. According to Mark's account, Jesus sent off two of his disciples to prepare the Passover meal for himself and his disciples. As they shared the meal together that evening Jesus gave the bread and wine a special meaning:

ᶜᶜ While they were eating, Jesus took a piece of bread, gave a prayer of thanks, broke it, and gave it to his disciples. "Take it," he said, "this is my body."

Then he took a cup, gave thanks to God, and handed it to them; and they all drank from it. Jesus said, "This is my blood which is poured out for many." ᵓᵓ
[Mark 14 : 22 – 24]

This is a modern sculpture by Colin Wilbourn called "The Upper Room", which refers to the room where Jesus and his disciples held the Last Supper.
▶ *What do you think the artist is trying to say about the Last Supper?*

"Do this in memory of me"

Luke adds that Jesus commanded the disciples to remember him by repeating this action. When they broke the bread they were to be reminded of his body which was to be broken on the cross. The pouring of the wine stood for the spilling of his blood.

Today Jesus' command is obeyed by Christians in churches throughout the world. Nearly all churches have a special service at which they eat the bread and drink the wine. The service is called by different names: Holy Communion, Mass, the Eucharist, the Liturgy. One boy said, "Going to Mass is very special to me. It reminds me of how much Jesus loves us – enough to die for us."

At the end of the meal they sang a hymn and went to the Mount of Olives, to a place called Gethsemane. Jesus told his disciples, "Sit here while I pray." He went a little further on, threw himself on the ground and prayed. "Father, my Father! All things are possible for you. Take this cup of suffering away from me. Yet not what I want, but what you want."
(Mark 14:32 – 36)

Gethsemane was a private garden. Jesus went there because it was a quiet place to pray. But it was also easy for his enemies to seek him out and arrest him there. In his prayer he argues with God. Jesus does not want to die, but he is willing to do God's will. There is a battle going on within Jesus' heart and mind.

The Agony in the Garden *by William Blake, painted around 1800. Blake painted this to show the struggle between Jesus and God.*

▶ *What do you think they are struggling about?*

---

1 *What special meals do you have? What makes a meal special?*

2 *If you had to invent a ceremony so that people could remember you when you were dead, what would it be? Explain your choice.*

3 *Which two symbols were used in the Last Supper? What do the two symbols represent at the Last Supper?*

4 *In pairs sit back to back. One of you is Jesus, the other is God the Father. Have a silent conversation by passing a piece of paper back to each other. Jesus starts off with the sentence, "It is dark. I am frightened..." He completes the sentence and then passes it to God. God has to convince him that there is no way but through death. When the conversation is finished you could read it out to the rest of the class.*

TWENTY-FIVE

JESUS IS BETRAYED

This unit looks at the story of Jesus' betrayal by Judas Iscariot, one of his disciples.

 (a) *Have you ever been betrayed or let down by a friend? What did it feel like? Did you forgive them? Explain your answer.*

(b) *Why do people betray each other? Make a list of reasons.*

When Jesus and his disciples were in Jerusalem for the feast of Passover, Judas went to the chief priests in order to betray Jesus to them. They were pleased to hear what he had to say, and promised to give him money – Matthew's Gospel says it was thirty silver coins. Judas then started to look for a good chance to hand Jesus over to them. The opportunity came when Jesus was in the garden of Gethsemane.

The Betrayal *by Stanley Spencer (painted in 1923).*

66 Jesus was still speaking when a crowd arrived, led by Judas, one of the twelve disciples. He came up to Jesus to kiss him. But Jesus said, "Judas, is it with a kiss that you betray the Son of Man?"

When the disciples who were with Jesus saw what was going to happen, they asked, "Shall we use our swords, Lord?" And one of them struck the High Priest's slave and cut off his right ear.

But Jesus said, "Enough of this!" He touched the man's ear and healed him.

Then Jesus said to the chief priests and the officers of the temple guard and the elders who had come there to get him. "Did you have to come with swords and clubs, as though I were an outlaw? I was with you in the Temple every day, and you did not try to arrest me. But this is your hour to act, when the power of darkness rules." 99

[Luke 22:47–53]

About the painter

Stanley Spencer (1891–1959) painted many scenes from the life of Jesus, and set most of them as if they were taking place in the village of Cookham, on the River Thames, where he lived. For Spencer, the events in Jesus' life were somehow happening again in Cookham. Spencer was trying to show that the life of Jesus was not just a historical event that happened 2000 years ago, but was actually relevant to people living in his village.

The artist has set the betrayal in the alleyway behind the corrugated-iron schoolroom at the bottom of his family's garden. He and his brother are watching from the wall.
Who are the other people? What exactly is happening? For clues, look at the passage from Luke opposite, Mark 14:50 and John 18:6.

 Write a guide to the painting, using the biblical account to help you. Explain who the characters are and what is happening, what emotions you think are present in the painting and why you think the artist set it in his own village. How does Spencer create an eerie effect? End by saying whether you think the painting helps you to understand the biblical story better, and explain why or why not.

Why did Judas betray Jesus?

The Gospels do not answer this question. There could have been a number of reasons:

- For money.
- Because he felt let down by Jesus. Judas may have expected Jesus to be the kind of Messiah who would defeat the Romans. (One explanation of his second name "Iscariot" links it to the sicarii, "assassins", who killed Romans.)
- Because he had arranged the meeting in the garden of Gethsemane with the hope of bringing Jesus and the authorities together. He may have been upset with Jesus' challenge to them, but not have realised how corrupt the authorities were. When the meeting went wrong he may have realised that he had betrayed Jesus.
- Because he knew Jesus would be arrested anyway and he wanted to save his own skin.

 (a) *Which reasons do you think are the most convincing, and the least convincing? Why?*
(b) *Did any of the other disciples let Jesus down? (Look up Matthew 26:69–75.)*
(c) *What happened to Judas? Read Matthew 27:3–5. Does it change your ideas about why he betrayed Jesus?*

Imagine that you are a film director who has been commissioned to make a film about the events leading up to the death of Jesus. The title of the film is The Traitor. *You have to put Jesus' betrayal in a modern-day setting. In small groups:*
(a) *Describe the scene in which this event would take place.*
(b) *Write a character sketch for the main actors in the drama. You should explain what they might be feeling in this scene to help the actors play it.*

TWENTY-SIX

N TRIAL

In this unit you will find out what happened after Jesus was arrested. You will also consider whether he got a fair trial and why he was condemned to death. Do any crimes today deserve the death penalty?

The Gospels give different accounts of the arrest and trial of Jesus. It is agreed that he was questioned in the early hours of Friday morning by members of the Sanhedrin (the Jewish religious council) and then by Pontius Pilate, the Roman Governor. The Sanhedrin tried to bring a case against Jesus that would put him to death. The Sadducees, the Jewish leaders, were desperate to get rid of Jesus once and for all.

The interrogations

1 By the Sanhedrin (the Council) The charge: blasphemy

The Sanhedrin had called in witnesses to provide evidence against Jesus, but none of their stories agreed (Mark 14:55 – 59).

> Again the High Priest questioned him, "Are you the Messiah, the Son of the Blessed God?"
>
> "I am," answered Jesus, "and you will all see the Son of Man seated on the right of the Almighty and coming with the clouds of heaven!"
>
> The High Priest tore his robes and said, "We don't need any more witnesses! You heard his blasphemy. What is your decision?"
>
> They all voted against him: he was guilty and should be put to death.
>
> [Mark 14:61 – 64]

But it is thought that only the Roman Governor could sentence somebody to death in the Roman Empire. He was therefore taken to Pontius Pilate.

2 By Pontius Pilate (the Roman Governor) The charge: rebellion against Rome

The religious leaders knew that Pilate would not be interested in a charge of blasphemy, therefore they said there were political reasons for condemning Jesus. Luke's Gospel (Luke 23:1 – 5) says the Jewish authorities now accused Jesus of:
- telling people not to pay their taxes to the Roman Emperor
- claiming to be king
- trying to cause a riot.

 Do you think any of these charges were reasonable? (Look up, for example, Matthew 22:15 – 21.)

When Pilate questioned Jesus he could not find anything which would justify the death penalty. He wanted to let him go.

Herod Antipas

Luke's Gospel then says that when Pilate heard Jesus was from Galilee he decided to pass him over to the ruler of Galilee, Herod Antipas (ruled 4 BCE – 39 CE), who was in Jerusalem at that time for the Passover. Herod was disliked by the Jews and was not trusted. Luke says he treated Jesus as a joke. He had his soldiers play games with him – they put a fine robe on him and mocked him, then sent him back to Pilate.

But the chief priests were determined that Jesus should die. It was the custom at Passover for the Governor to release one prisoner asked for by the crowd. A crowd had gathered for the release of the prisoner. Matthew says that the chief priests persuaded the crowd to ask for a man named Barabbas to be set free and for Jesus to be put to death:

3 *In groups discuss what happens in a court of law today. Who is in the court? What type of evidence is needed to convict someone? Who finds the person guilty or innocent? How is fairness maintained? Was the trial of Jesus fair?*

This is an engraving of Jesus before Pilate by Georges Rouault (1871–1958), who was a devout Christian.
▶ *What do you think this picture is saying?*

66 Pilate asked the crowd,
   "Which one of these two do you want me to set free for you?"
"Barabbas!" they answered.
"What, then, shall I do with Jesus called the Messiah?" Pilate asked them.
"Crucify him!" they all answered. 99
[Matthew 27:21 – 22]

2 *Did Pilate have a choice? What might have happened if he'd refused to set Barabbas free? (Look up, for example, Matthew 27:24.)*

On 7 April 1995 Nick Ingram (31) was executed in the United States for the murder of a 61-year-old man during a burglary. Death by electrocution means that the body burns from the inside. It is a horrific form of torture.
▶ *What does this account make you feel? Do you think this is a humane way of punishing somebody?*
▶ *Do you think that any crimes deserve the death penalty. If so, which ones?*

TWENTY-SEVEN

JESUS IS CRUCIFIED

This unit looks at the mocking and crucifixion of Jesus, and considers how two different painters understood the event.

Crucifixion

Crucifixion was a common Roman punishment. Before the victim was put on the cross he would be whipped with a scourge (a whip with sharp bones knotted in). Death could take hours or even days. The victim died through suffocation, when he became too tired to push up with his arms to catch breath. Jesus was placed on the cross at nine o'clock in the morning. He died only six hours later.

Narrator: The soldiers put a purple robe on Jesus, made a crown of thorny branches, and put it on his head. They began to salute him:

Soldiers: Long live the King of the Jews!

Narrator: They beat him over the head with a stick, spat on him, fell on their knees, and bowed down to him. When they had finished mocking him, they took off the purple robe and put his own clothes back on him. Then they led him out to crucify him.

[Mark 15:17–21]

Narrator: Two other men, both of them criminals, were also led out to be put to death with Jesus. When they came to the place called "The Skull" they crucified Jesus there, and the two other criminals, one on his right and the other on his left. Jesus said:

Jesus: Forgive them Father! They don't know what they are doing.

Narrator: They divided his clothes among themselves by throwing dice. The people stood there watching while the Jewish leaders jeered at him.

Leader 1: He saved others, let him save himself!

Leader 2: If he is the Messiah, whom God has chosen!

. . .

Narrator: Above him were written these words:

Pilate: This is the King of the Jews.

. . .

Narrator: It was about twelve o'clock when the sun stopped shining and darkness covered the whole country until three o'clock, and the curtain hanging in the Temple was torn in two. Jesus cried out in a loud voice:

Jesus: Father! Into your hands I place my spirit!

Narrator: He said this and died.

[Luke 23:32–35, 38, 44–46]

1. (a) What is another word for "mocked"? List all the ways in which Jesus was mocked.
   (b) Why do you think the Roman soldiers mocked Jesus?

This is an early sixteenth-century painting of the Crucifixion by the German artist Mathias Grünewald.

▶ Imagine you have just seen this painting in an art gallery. Write a paragraph or a poem describing it. Say what it makes you feel and what you think the artist was trying to say.

▶ If you had to choose one of Jesus' "last words" as a title for Grünewald's painting, which would you choose? Explain why.

In 1985 Brian Keenan was taken hostage and tortured by terrorists. In his autobiography *An Evil Cradling* he describes the experience of being tortured by a man called Said:

> 66 Said began by taking deep breaths, deeper and deeper, faster and faster . . . I sat and listened to him exciting himself into violence. Down it came, hard on my shoulders, driving into my chest. Then along my thighs, banging against my knees . . . Every part of my body was being insulted . . . In that moment I hated him, I did not fear him. 99

2. (a) Why do you think people torture others?
   (b) How did Brian Keenan react under torture? How did Jesus react under torture?

The Gospels record that Jesus spoke a number of words from the cross. Here are some of them:

▶ *"Forgive them, Father! They don't know what they are doing."* (Luke 23:34)
▶ *"Father! In your hands I place my spirit!"* (Luke 23:46)
▶ *"My God, my God, why did you abandon me?"* (Mark 15:34)
▶ *"It is finished!"* (John 19:30)

3. For Christians Jesus is both human and divine (God). Which of these paintings (a) shows him to be human, (b) shows him to be divine?

4. Christians believe that when Jesus died on the cross he was showing his love for all people. This love was costly. Think of examples when it has been difficult to show someone love. Why has it been costly? How do parents sometimes show this love to their children?

Part of Albrecht Dürer's painting of The Adoration of the Trinity (1511).

▶ How does Dürer's painting of the crucifixion differ from Grünewald's?

▶ Which of Jesus' "last words" would you choose as a title? Explain why.

TWENTY-EIGHT

E HAS BEEN RAISED"

What do you think happens after death? In this unit you will find out what Christians believe happened to Jesus after his death.

Jesus was taken down from the cross on Friday, before sunset, and placed in a tomb cut into the side of a hill. This is what Luke's Gospel says happened next:

> " Very early on Sunday morning the women went to the tomb carrying the spices they had prepared. They found the stone rolled away from the entrance to the tomb, so they went in; but they did not find the body of the Lord Jesus. They stood there puzzled about this, when suddenly two men in bright shining clothes stood by them. Full of fear, the women bowed down to the ground, as the men said to them, "Why are you looking among the dead for one who is alive? He is not here; he has been raised. Remember what he said to you while he was in Galilee: 'The Son of Man must be handed over to sinful man, be crucified, and three days later rise to life.' "
>
> [Luke 24:1 – 7]

1 *The four Gospels give different accounts of the finding of the empty tomb.*

(a) Imagine you are journalists for The Jerusalem News *and you have been told to interview one of the women who found the tomb empty. Divide into four groups and take one of the Gospel accounts each: Matthew 28:1 – 10; Mark 16:1 – 8; Luke 24:1 – 12; John 20:1 – 2, 11 – 18. Prepare the questions you are going to ask, such as asking her name, who was with her, what she did, what she heard and felt etc. Then write her answers using your Gospel account as a basis. You could then read out your report or role-play it to the other groups.*

(b) Discuss the differences. Why do you think they are different?

Did you know?
Jesus' body would have been laid on a stone shelf inside a cave. It would be left there until only the bones remained. Then, maybe a year later, the bones would be put into a small casket, called an "ossuary", so that the tomb could be used for another body.

Some people find it difficult to believe that Jesus rose from the dead. They explain the disappearance of the body in different ways, for example:

▶ Jesus did not actually die. He became unconscious on the cross and later recovered in the tomb.

▶ The disciples stole the body and later told people that he had been raised from the dead.

▶ The women went to the wrong tomb.

In groups take each of these theories in turn. Make a list of the arguments you can think up (a) in support of the theory, and (b) against the theory. Use the last chapters of each of the Gospels to help you, e.g. Matthew 28:11 – 15.

During the next forty days the Gospels and other books in the New Testament say that the risen Jesus appeared to many of his followers. He taught his disciples that they were to continue his work on earth and that his death and resurrection were part of God's plan.

3 *Christians celebrate the Resurrection at Easter. Devise and carry out a questionnaire to find out how Christians celebrate Easter today. Write up your findings, include pictures if you can.*

This is a modern painting, Christ and His Cross, by José Clemente Orozco.
- ▶ *What is the artist trying to say in painting the picture in this way?*
- ▶ *Compare it with Grünewald's picture on page 57. How do they differ?*
- ▶ *Give the painting your own title.*

TWENTY-NINE

ESUS' INFLUENCE TODAY

In this unit you will learn about the influence which Jesus has upon people today.

The community of disciples who followed Jesus has today spread into a worldwide religion. He is worshipped as the Son of God in Christian churches all over the globe. Christians claim that he has affected or helped them in many ways. The athlete Kris Akabusi said:

> "" Jesus has given a new meaning to my life. When I read all the things the Bible says about Jesus I knew I had a decision to make. I started investigating to find out if it was really true. In California I made a decision to give my life to Jesus Christ. I had a good time before I became a Christian but I'm having a better time now. When I became a Christian I stopped having to prove that I was as good as everyone else. ""

Margery Wilson's son died of cancer in the brain:

> "" I felt great pain when I watched Earl die. But I believe there is another world – you just open the door and you're with Jesus and you are out of all pain and suffering. ""

Jesus' teaching has also inspired people to live selfless lives working for others. Two examples are shown on the next page.

Kris Akabusi in action

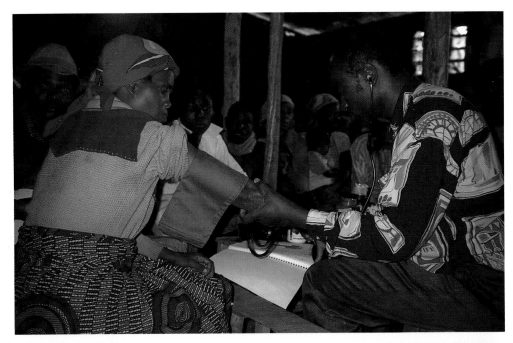

Christian Aid supports medical work all around the world.

Jean Vanier left a highly successful job as a professor in Canada to dedicate his life to working and living with handicapped people in the L'Arche (The Ark) community he founded. He was imitating Jesus when he especially showed love to outcasts in society. Today there are L'Arche communities all over the world.

1 Find out about the Christian work of one of the following organisations:
CAFOD
Tear Fund
Christian Aid
Operation Christmas Child
The Samaritans
Write up your findings in the form of a leaflet or wall-chart explaining what the organisation does and how it is based on the teachings of Jesus.

2 At the beginning of this book you were asked to give at least two reasons for finding out about Jesus. As a class, having read this book, add any more reasons you can think of. Then hold a debate: "Only Christians should learn about Jesus."

GLOSSARY

Apostle One who was "sent out" by Jesus to preach the **Gospel**

Baptism Religious ceremony when a person is immersed in, or sprinkled with, water. In Christianity it shows a person has become a member of the Christian Church

Christian A follower of "Christ", a title which Jesus' followers gave him. See also **Messiah**

Christmas Christian festival (25 December) which celebrates the birth of Jesus

Crucifixion Roman method of executing criminals and traitors by fastening them to a cross

Devil, the Also referred to as Satan. The spirit of evil; the enemy of God; the tempter of people

Disciple A follower of Jesus

Easter The main Christian festival (in March or April) which celebrates the **resurrection** of Jesus

Exorcism Casting out of evil spirits

Gospel "Good news". The preaching of Jesus; also the accounts of his life by Matthew, Mark, Luke and John

Holy Spirit Christians believe God's Spirit is active in every Christian life and in the world

Incarnation The belief that God became a human person in Jesus

Kingdom of God The reign of God; a time of peace and blessing

Last Supper The last meal Jesus had with his disciples. It is remembered by Christians today in their main church service, which has different names, including Mass, Eucharist, Breaking the Bread

Law, the The first five books of the Old Testament and the hundreds of commandments that they contain. Moses was once thought to be the author of all five books (see Unit 21)

Messiah A person chosen by God for a special task. Used in the Jewish tradition to refer to the expected leader sent by God to save his people. Jesus' followers applied this title to him – in Greek the word for Messiah is "Christ"

Ministry Refers to Jesus' public work after his baptism

Miracle Normally used of occurrences that cannot be explained by the laws of nature

Nativity The birth of Jesus

New Testament Collection of twenty-seven books that form the second part of the Christian Bible. The first four books are the Gospels

Old Testament Collection of thirty-nine books that form the first part of the Christian Bible, e.g. Deuteronomy, Isaiah. These are also the Scriptures of the Jews

Palm Sunday The Sunday before **Easter**, remembering the entry of Jesus into Jerusalem when the crowds waved palm branches

Parable A story or short saying that uses everyday events to give a religious meaning

Passover Jewish festival celebrating the time when God helped the Jewish people to escape from slavery in Egypt

Prophet A person who speaks on behalf of God

Rabbi "My teacher"

Resurrection The rising from the dead of Jesus Christ, celebrated at **Easter**

Sabbath Jewish day of rest (Friday sunset to Saturday sunset)

Sanhedrin The supreme Jewish council at the time of Jesus

Scripture For Christians this means the Old and New Testaments. When it is used in the New Testament (e.g. by Jesus) it means the Old Testament

Sermon on the Mount A collection of Jesus' teachings (Matthew chapters 5 – 7)

Son of Man Jesus often used this title of himself. Its meaning is vague – perhaps this is one of the reasons why Jesus used it of himself. It could mean "a human being" or "a heavenly being". Jesus often talked about the suffering son of man

Synagogues Places of study, worship and meeting for Jews at the time of Jesus. Today it is the name given to buildings used by Jews for public prayer, study and community meetings

Transfiguration The event when Jesus' appearance altered and shone with light (see Unit 21)

INDEX

ACKNOWLEDGEMENTS

The author would like to thank Mark Brimicombe and Monica Kendall for helpful suggestions during the preparation of the book for publication. The author and publishers would also like to thank the following for permission to reproduce photographs:

Ace Photo Agency: p28; Colin Alston: p50; Andes Press Agency/Carlos Rayes Marizo: pp31, 46; L'Arche: p61(top); Barnaby's Picture Library: pps 11, 19; Bettmann Archive: p55(bottom); Bridgeman Art Library: pp6, 21(bottom), 23 (top), 25, 49, 51, 52, 57; Lorraine Calaora: p17; Christian Aid: p61(bottom); CIRCA Photo Library/ICOREC: p41; Collections/Ben Boswell: p21(top); Format Partners/Miriam Reik: p18; Sonia Halliday Photographs: pps 7(bottom), 48 (bottom); Hood Museum of Art/Commissioned by the Trustees of Dartmouth College, Hanover, New Hampshire: p59; Hulton Deutsch Collection Ltd: pp9, 10; Life File/Mike Evans: p20; Life File/Richard Powers: p47; Lilly Library, Indiana University: p55(top); Misereor Medienproduktion und Vretriebsgesellschaft mbH, Aachen, Germany (Ethiopian Lenten Veil, Alemayehu Bizuneh): pp26, 27, 42; Network Photographers Ltd: p23(bottom); Rex Features Ltd: p29; Rex Features Ltd/Stipa Press: pp33(left), 48(top); Rex Features Ltd/Stipa Press/Luc Delahaye: p33(right); Sporting Pictures (UK) Ltd: p60; Ateliers et Presses de Taizé: p45; Vatican Library, Rome: p16; Vie de Jesus Mafa: p7(top).

Cover photo of African Jesus: CIRCA Photo Library/ ICOREC

Grateful acknowledgement is also made for permission to use extracts from the *Good News Bible*:

Scriptures quoted from the Good News Bible published by The Bible Societies/Harper Collins Publishers, UK © American Bible Society 1966, 1971, 1976, 1992 used with permission.

Good News Bible dramatised texts from *"The Dramatised Bible"*
© 1989 Michael Perry, text © 1966, 1971, 1976 American Bible Society.

Artwork was provided by:
Roger Backwell p31; Tony Chance pp24, 34, 35, 38; Robert Goldsmith pp12, 32, 33, 40; Colin MacNeil pp14, 36, 37; Chris Molan pp4, 5, 8, 9.

Oxford University Press, Walton St, Oxford, OX2 6DP

Oxford   New York
Athens   Auckland   Bangkok   Bogota   Bombay
Buenos Aires   Calcutta   Cape Town   Dar es Salaam
Delhi   Florence   HongKong   Istanbul   Karachi
Kuala Lumpur   Madras   Madrid   Melbourne
Mexico City   Nairobi   Paris   Singapore   Taipei
Tokyo   Toronto

and associated companies in
Berlin   Ibadan

Oxford is a trade mark of Oxford University Press
© Oxford University Press

First published in 1996

ISBN 0 19 917239 0

A CIP catalogue record for this book is available from the British Library.

Printed and bound in Hong Kong.